THE UNIVERSE

THE MOON

ABDO
Publishing Company

A Buddy Book **by Fran Howard**

VISIT US AT

www.abdopublishing.com

Published by ABDO Publishing Company, 8000 West 78th Street, Edina, Minnesota 55439.

Printed in the United States.

Editor: Sarah Tieck
Contributing Editor: Michael P. Goecke
Graphic Design: Maria Hosley
Cover Image: Photos.com
Interior Images: Library of Congress (page 23); Lushpix (page 11); NASA (page 25, 29); NASA: Glen Research Center (page 13), Jet Propulsion Laboratory (page 7, 13), JPL / Space Science Institute (page 7), Johnson Space Center (page 30); Photos.com (page 5, 15, 21, 26, 27).

Library of Congress Cataloging-in-Publication Data

Howard, Fran, 1953-
   The moon / Fran Howard.
      p. cm. — (The universe)
   Includes index.
   ISBN 978-1-59928-929-8
   1. Moon—Juvenile literature. I. Title.

QB582.H69 2008
523.3—dc22
                              2007027786

Table Of Contents

What Is The Moon?

When people look up into the night sky, they can see thousands of stars. Sometimes, they can even see planets glowing brightly. Earth's moon is another common sight in the sparkling night sky.

The moon is about one-fourth the size of Earth. It is the second-brightest object in our sky after our sun.

5

Our Solar System

The moon is part of our solar system. A solar system is a single star with space objects, such as planets, orbiting it. Our sun is the center of our solar system.

Earth is one of eight planets that orbit our sun. The other planets are Mercury, Venus, Mars, Jupiter, Saturn, Uranus, and Neptune. Three dwarf planets also orbit the sun. Pluto is one dwarf planet.

Some planets have moons. So far, scientists have discovered more than 100 moons in our solar system.

Rhea is one of Saturn's moons.

Triton is Neptune's largest moon.

Deimos *(left)* and Phobos *(right)* are the two moons of Mars.

Ganymede is one of Jupiter's moons.

There are many different kinds of moons. They vary in size, shape, brightness, temperature, and color.

Many Moons

Any object orbiting a planet is considered a satellite. For instance, a **spacecraft** can be a satellite.

Our moon is a natural satellite. It orbits Earth. Earth's **gravity** holds the moon in place. The moon is Earth's only natural satellite.

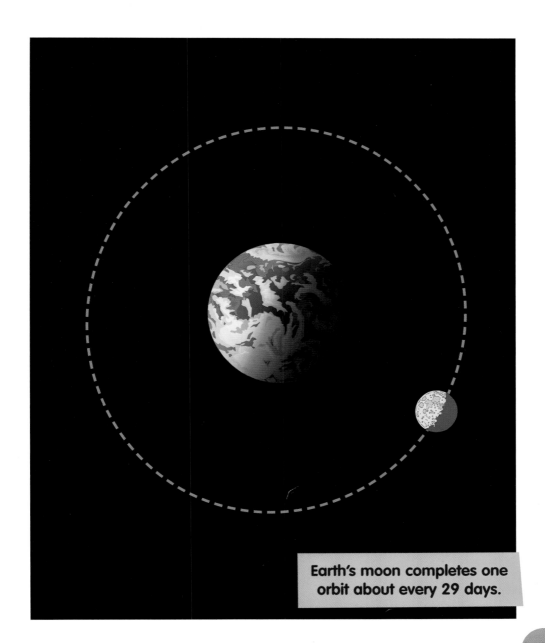

Earth's moon completes one orbit about every 29 days.

A Closer Look

The moon's surface is covered with large craters. The moon also has light and dark spots.

The light spots are **highlands**. The dark spots are called maria. Maria are **plains** that formed when **lava** flowed into craters. The lava came from within the moon long ago.

There are thousands of craters on the moon's surface. They formed when large objects crashed into the moon. The largest crater on the moon is 1,344 miles (2,163 km) wide. It is almost eight miles (13 km) deep!

Very small pieces of dust and rock cover the moon's surface. This layer probably formed when space objects hit the moon.

Scientists say the moon could contain small amounts of frozen water. There are deep craters that are always in darkness. Scientists believe the water ice might be found in them.

The moon's surface is full of small and large craters *(above right)*. Scientists have learned about the moon's surface with the help of lunar rovers *(below)*.

What Is It Like There?

The moon has very little **atmosphere**. Because of this, space objects do not burn up in the atmosphere's gases. Instead, they just hit the moon. This is why the moon has so many craters.

Atmospheres also help protect planets from temperature extremes. With so little atmosphere, the moon gets very cold and very hot. It has no wind. And, it does not rain or snow there.

Temperatures reach about 265 degrees Fahrenheit (130°C) on the side of the moon facing the sun. On the dark side of the moon, temperatures can fall to -280 degrees Fahrenheit (-173°C).

Beneath The Surface

Like Earth, the moon has a hard surface. This is the crust. Inside the moon are the mantle and the core.

The crust is the moon's outermost layer. It is made of light-colored rocky material.

The mantle is the moon's middle layer. It is mostly rocky with a few metals. **Moonquakes** occur deep within the mantle. These are caused by the moon's orbit around Earth.

The core is the innermost part of the moon. The moon's core and mantle are similar to those of Earth.

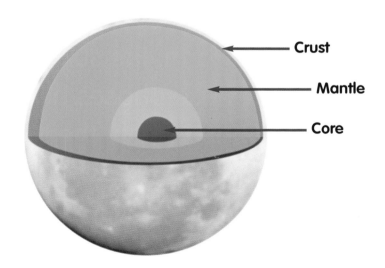

Crust

Mantle

Core

Different Phases

The moon moves through its **phases** about every 29 days. So from Earth, people see different amounts of the moon throughout this time period.

The moon's phases change with the movement of Earth, the sun, and the moon itself. These phases happen according to how Earth, the moon, and the sun line up.

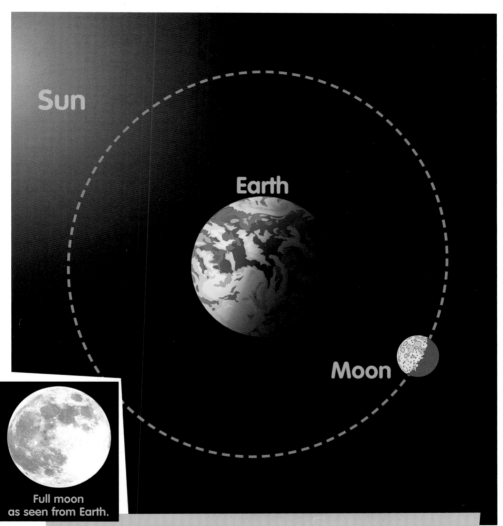

Full moon
as seen from Earth.

The moon is round and bright during a full moon. This occurs when Earth is between the moon and the sun.

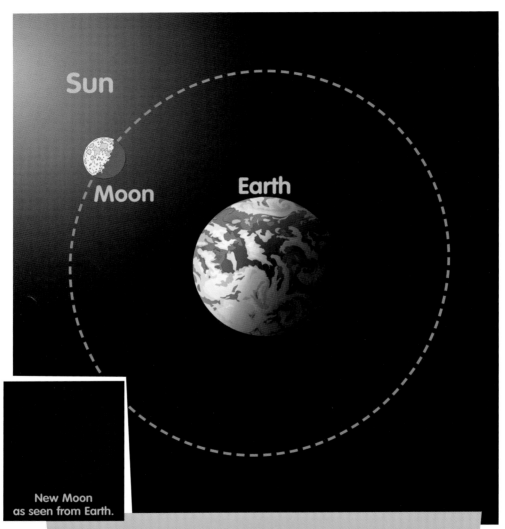

Sun

Moon

Earth

New Moon
as seen from Earth.

The moon is dark during the new moon phase. It happens
when the moon is between Earth and the sun.

First Quarter Moon

Gibbous Moon

Crescent Moon

Other moon phases include the first quarter moon,
the gibbous moon, and the crescent moon.

Discovering The Moon

People have always known about the moon. Many ancient people thought the moon was a goddess. The Romans named the moon after their goddess Luna.

Many people also thought the moon had a smooth surface. But in 1609, Italian scientist Galileo Galilei viewed the moon through a telescope. He discovered the moon had mountains and craters on its surface.

Galileo was famous for his ideas.
He lived from 1564 to 1642.

Missions To The Moon

The moon is the only space object humans have visited. The Soviet Union and the United States had a space race for many years.

In 1959, the Soviet Union's *Luna 2* became the first **spacecraft** to visit the moon. That same year, *Luna 3* took the first photographs of the moon's dark side.

In 1966, *Luna 9* became the first **spacecraft** to successfully land on the moon. That same year, *Luna 10* became the first unmanned spacecraft to orbit the moon.

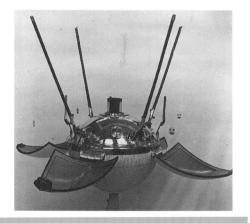

Luna 9 landed in a part of the moon called the Ocean of Storms. The spacecraft returned the first pictures from the moon's surface.

The United States won the space race in 1969. That year, a U.S. astronaut became the first person to walk on the moon. By 1972, 12 people had walked on the moon.

On July 21, 1969, Neil Armstrong became the first person to stand on the moon. He was part of the Apollo 11 mission. In total, 12 people have walked on the moon.

The Apollo and Luna missions brought pieces of moon rock back to Earth.

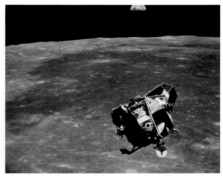

The moon is about 4.5 billion years old. Scientists believe it formed when a large space object hit Earth. Years later, broken pieces from this crash came together. Scientists say these pieces rejoined to form the moon.

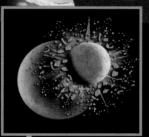
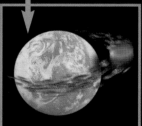

The giant impact theory describes how the moon formed. It suggests that an object as big as Mars hit Earth.

The Great Moon Hoax happened in 1835. A New York newspaper printed five articles describing moon plants and animals. The stories were not true, but they tricked many people!

Eugene Cernan is the most recent astronaut to stand on the moon. He was part of the Apollo 17 **mission** in December 1972.

Astronauts from Apollo 17 were the moon's most recent visitors. They traveled great distances across the surface and collected many samples.

Voyage To Tomorrow

People want to learn more about the moon. Many nations want to send **spacecraft** and people to the moon.

U.S. scientists developed the *Lunar Reconnaissance Orbiter*. It will map the moon's surface and search for water ice. The orbiter is expected to **launch** in 2008.

Also, India is planning its first unmanned moon **mission** for 2008.

In 2013, the Lunar South Polar Sample Return Mission will launch. This mission will collect moon rocks *(right)* and bring them to Earth.

Important Words

atmosphere the layer of gases that surrounds space objects, including planets, moons, and stars.

highland a mountainous region.

launch to send with force.

lava hot liquid rock that flows from the center of a volcano.

mission the sending of spacecraft to perform specific jobs.

moonquake sudden motion or trembling of the moon.

phase a regularly occurring stage of change.

plain large areas of flat land.

spacecraft a vehicle that travels in space.

Web Sites

To learn more about the **moon**, visit ABDO Publishing Company on the World Wide Web. Web sites about the **moon** are featured on our Book Links page. These links are routinely monitored and updated to provide the most current information available.

www.abdopublishing.com

INDEX